Change for the better
valspar

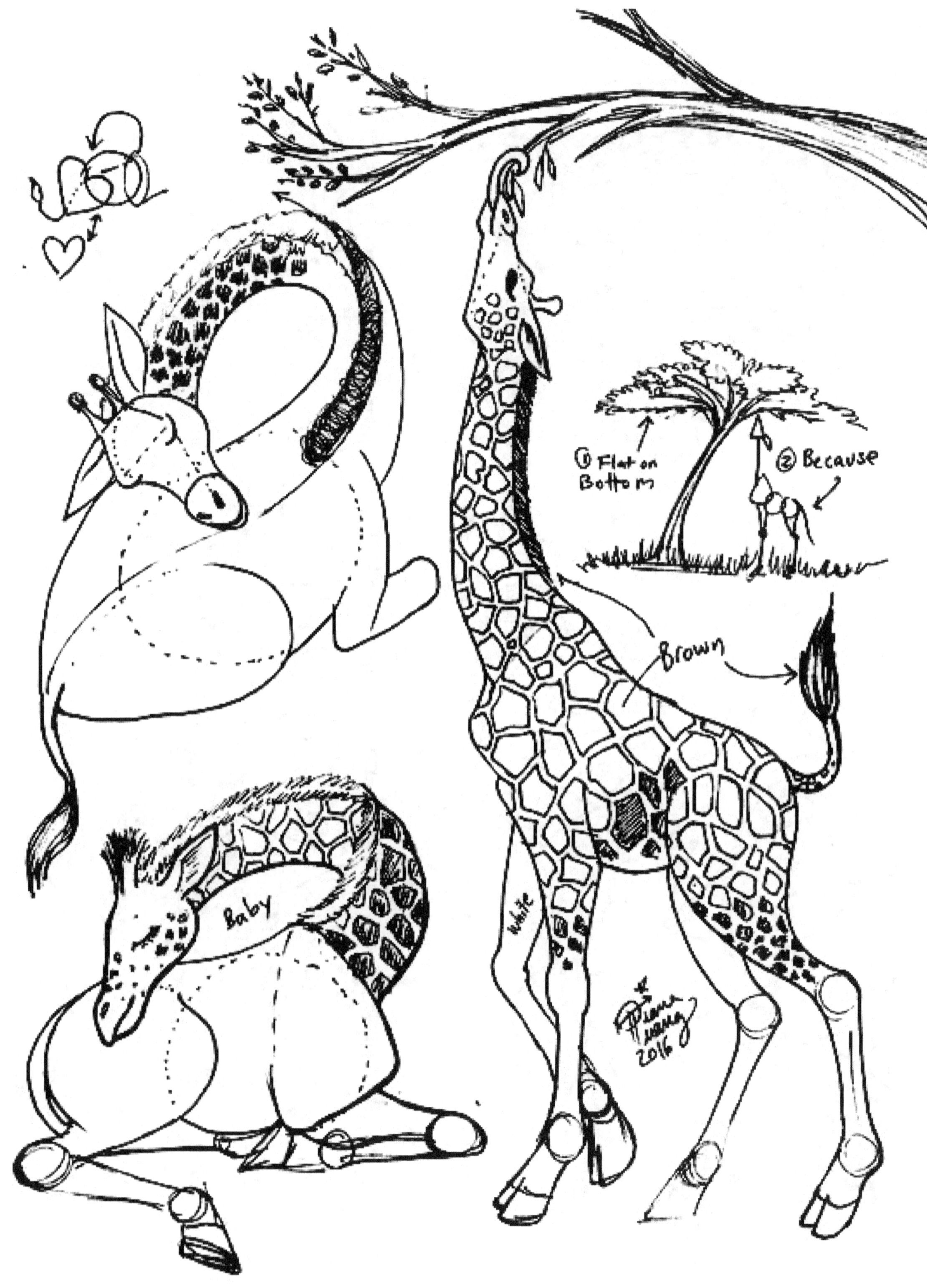

① Flat on Bottom
② Because
Brown
Baby
White
2016

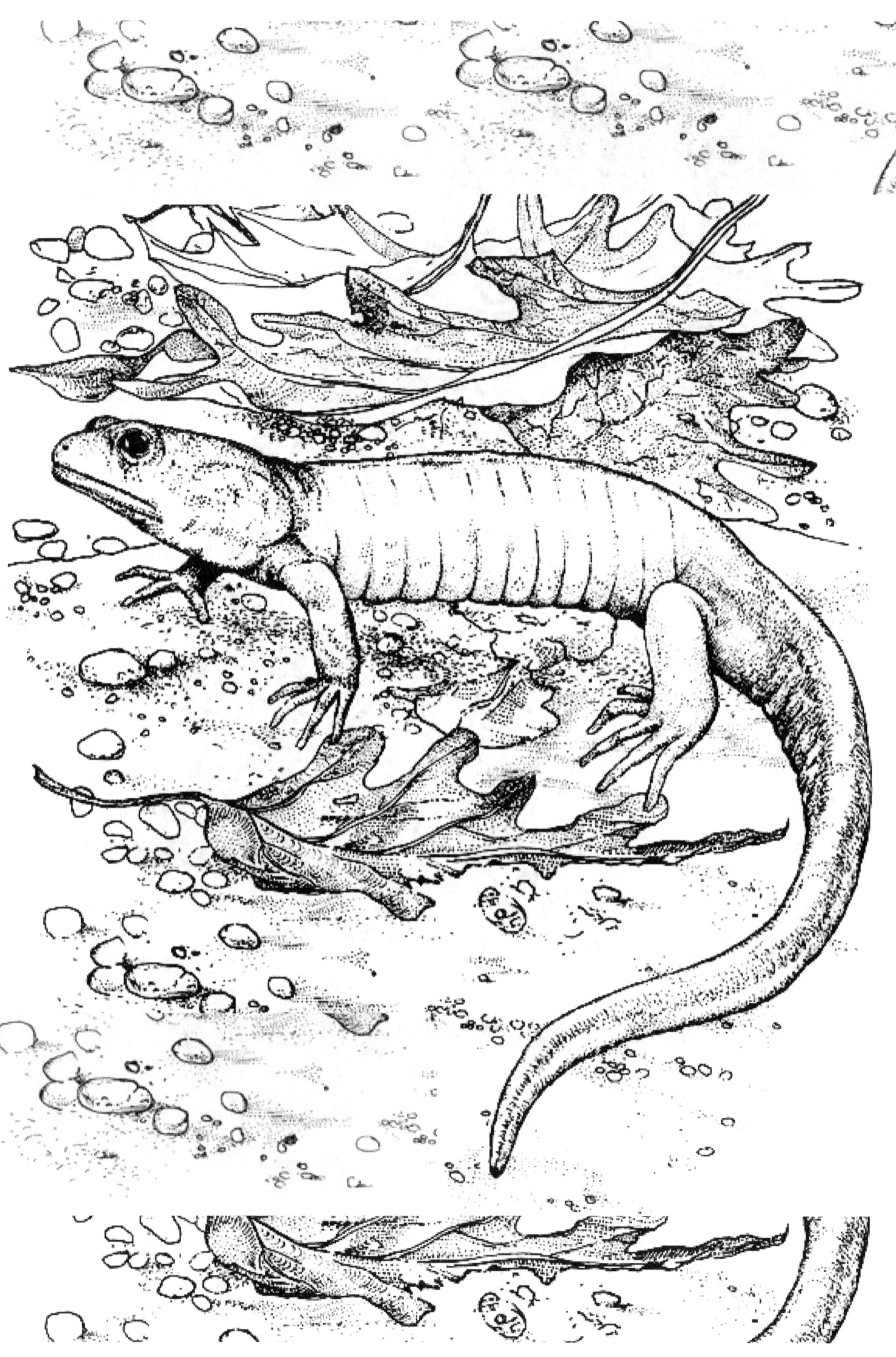

Animal
Camel

www.favoreads.club

paint the world
SUPER

What Big Feet You Have!
Copyright: Chabrier House of Chabrier 2012
Anne E. Shoemaker-Magdaleno
All Rights Reserved
CHABRIER • 4-17-2012

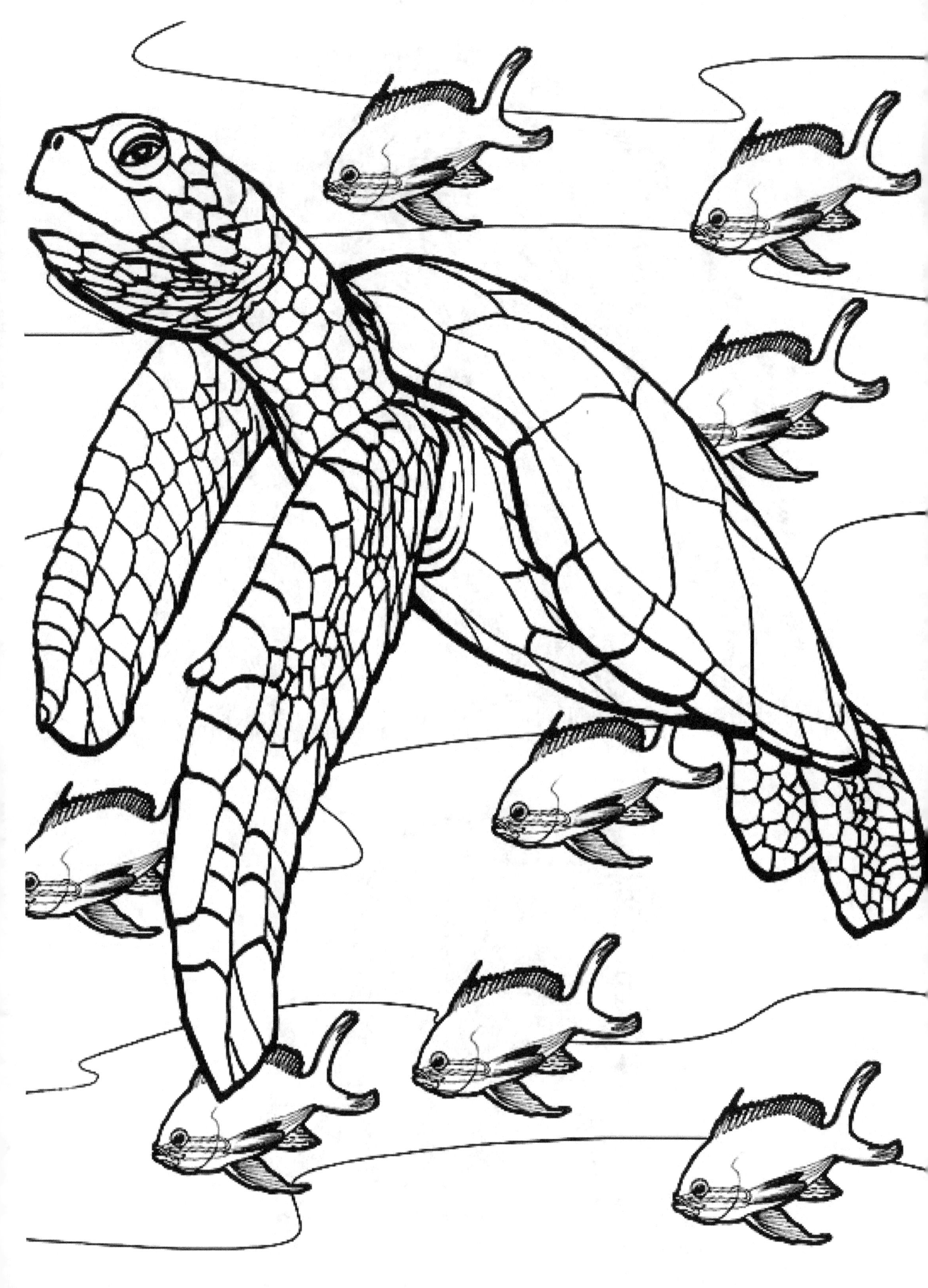

paint the world
SUPER
COLORING

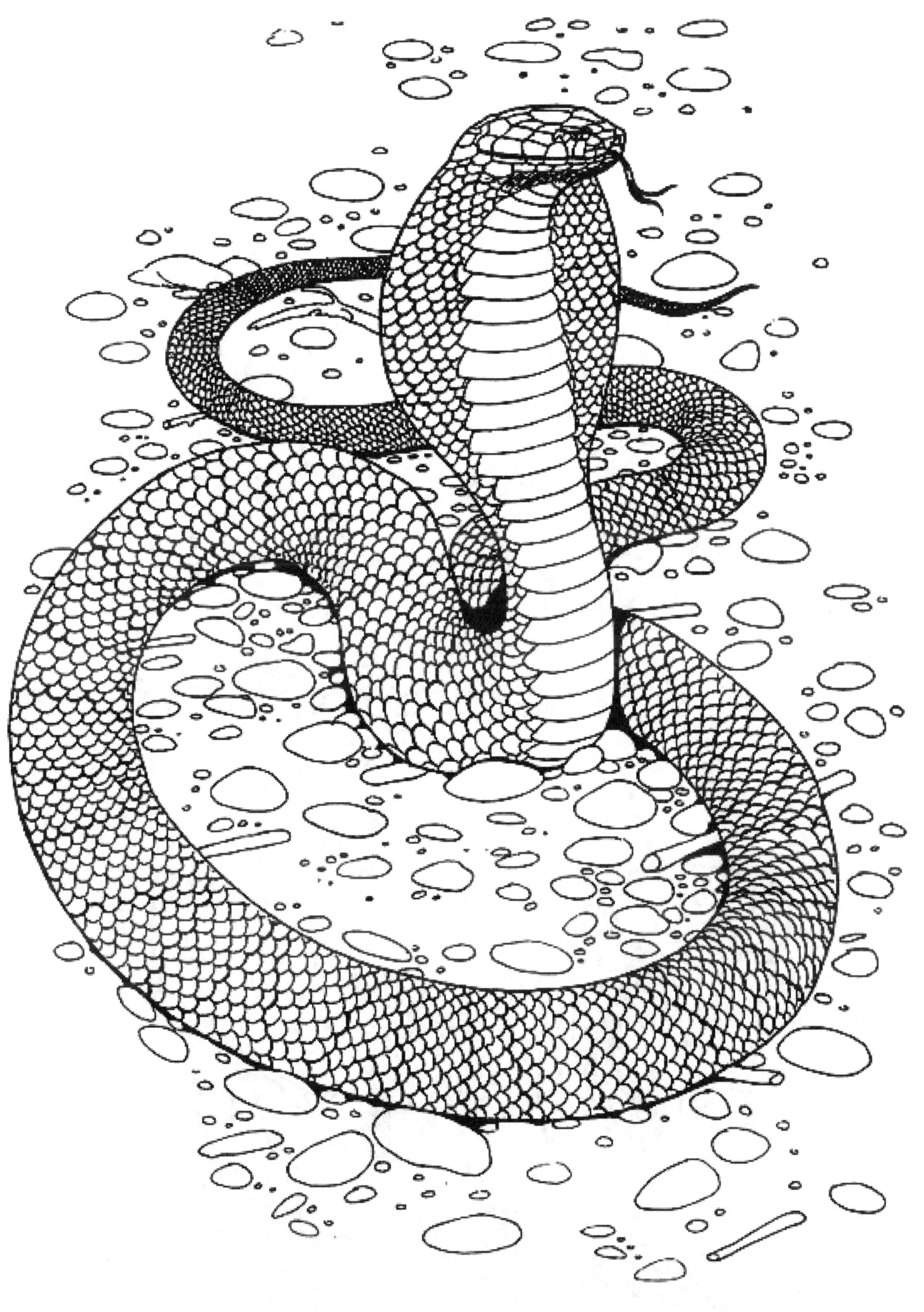

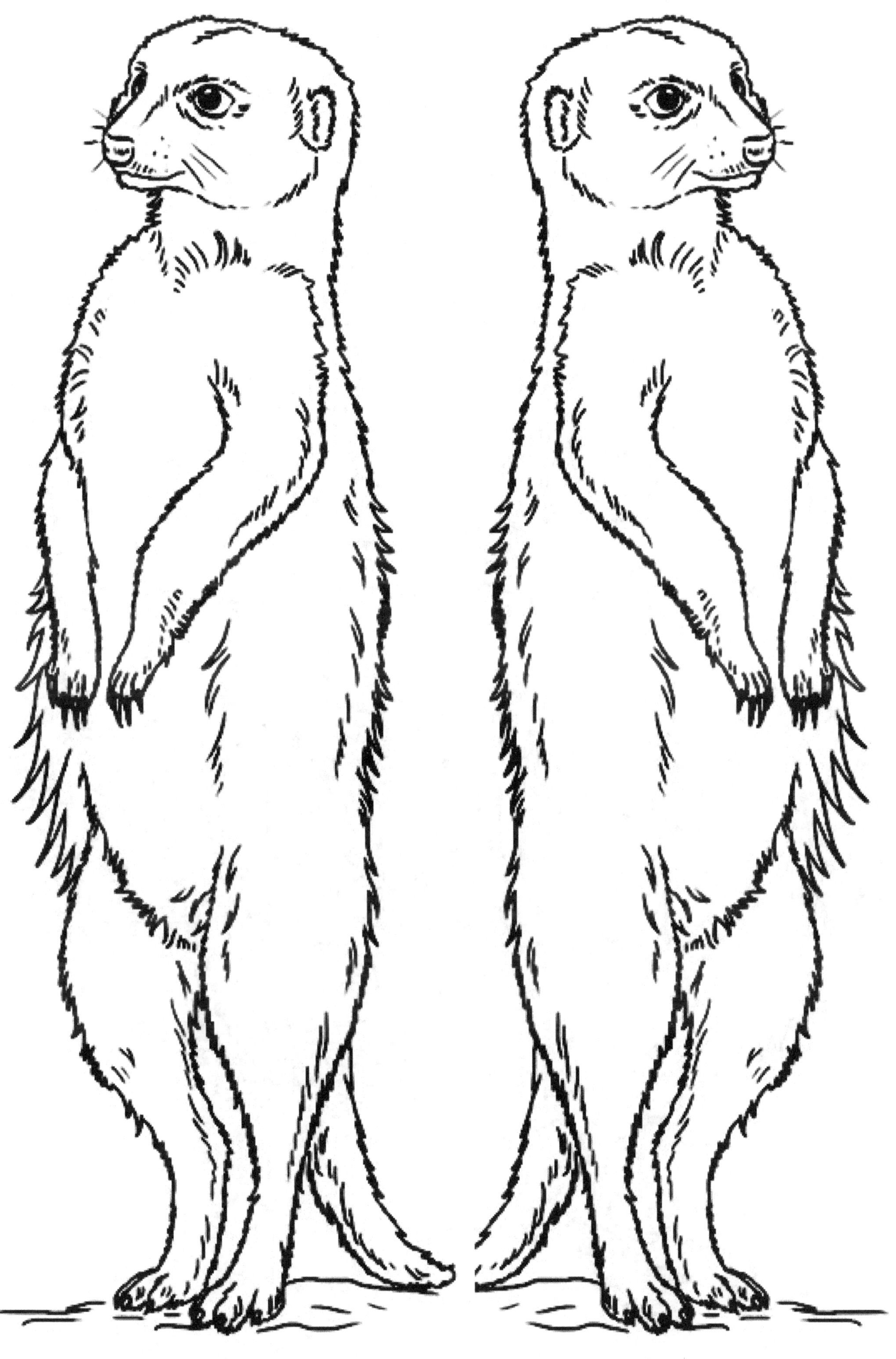

© Jill Buckley 2014

amberdog

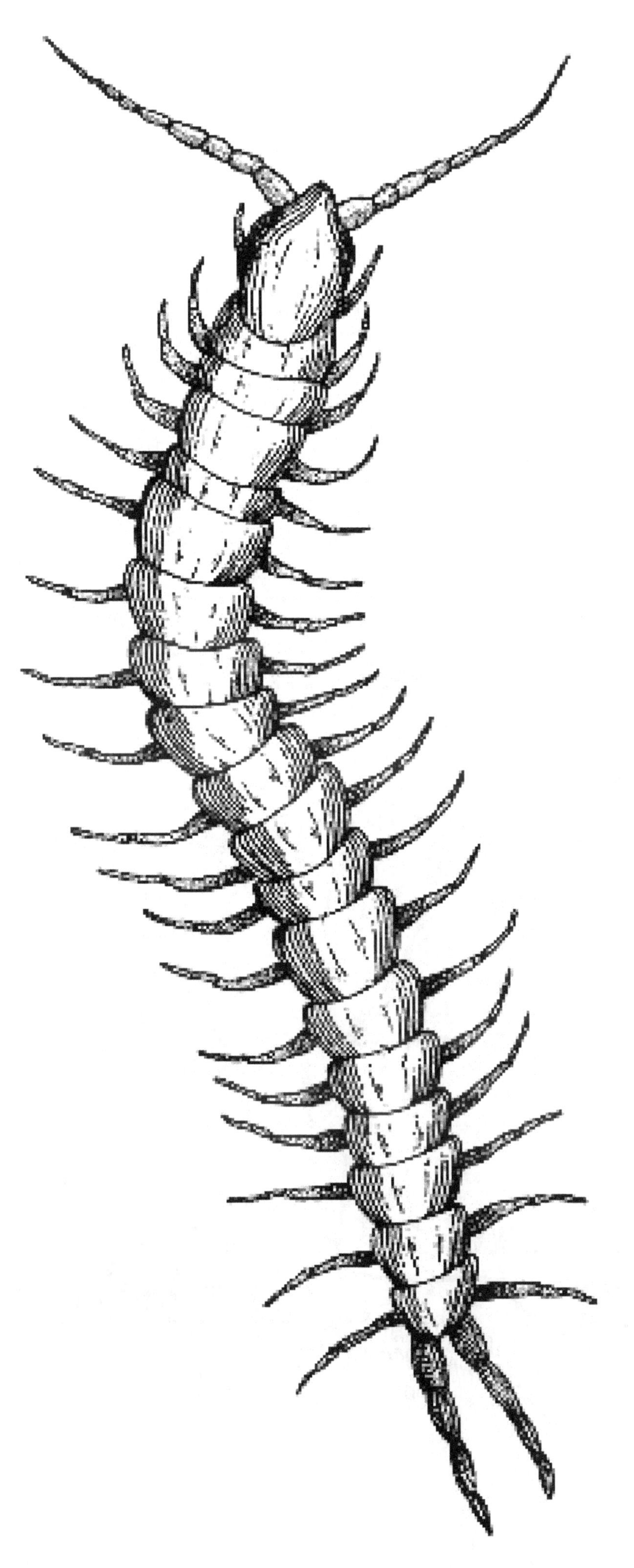

Zebras